In the Ocean

Jennifer Szymanski

NATIONAL GEOGRAPHIC

Washington, D.C.

How to Use This Book

Reading together is fun! When older and younger readers share the experience, it opens the door to new learning. As you read together, talk about what you learn.

YOU READ

This side is for a parent, older sibling, or older friend. Before reading each page, take a look at the words and pictures. Talk about what you see. Point out words that might be hard for the younger reader.

I READ

This side is for the younger reader.

As you read, look for the bolded words. Talk about them before you read. In each chapter, the bolded words are:
Chapter 1: ocean words • Chapter 2: places
Chapter 3: describing words • Chapter 4: action words

At the end of each chapter, do the activity together.

Table of Contents

Water in the Ocean

An ocean is a large body of **water**. Most of Earth is covered by oceans. They make our planet look blue from outer space.

From space, the oceans look still. They are not! Ocean **water** is always moving.

YOU READ

We can see ocean water moving by watching the tide. At high tide, water covers the **beach**.

I READ At low tide, the water moves back. Now we can see the **beach**!

YOU READ

Waves swell and crash in the ocean. Wind helps make waves. A fast wind that blows for a long time can create huge waves.

 Other times, **waves** are small. They rock back and forth.

YOUR TURN!

Move like the ocean!
Tell what you are doing.

CHAPTER 2

Ocean Homes

Many animals live in the ocean. Some live in tide **pools**. These pools are made from rocks near the shore. Water covers them when the tide is high.

 At low tide, the **pools** have less water. But animals still live there.

YOU READ

This **forest** doesn't have trees! It has kelp instead. The kelp here grows very tall to reach the sunlight.

Fish hide in the kelp's leaves. Otters dive into the **forest** to find food to eat.

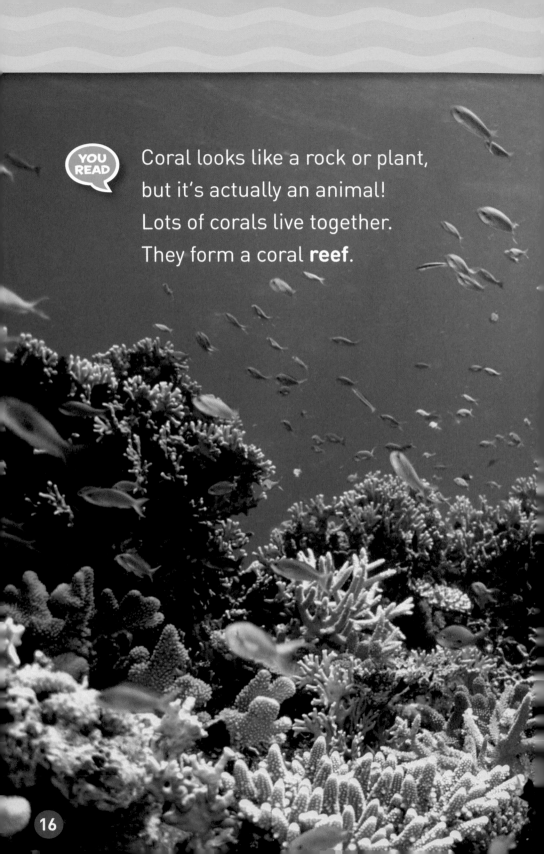

YOU READ Coral looks like a rock or plant, but it's actually an animal! Lots of corals live together. They form a coral **reef**.

I READ Coral **reefs** are home to many living things. Eels hide in the coral. It keeps them safe.

narwhals

It's tough to live in some ocean places. The North Pole is very cold all year. Much of the water and land is covered with **ice**. But animals still live there.

The South Pole has **ice**, too! Feathers help these penguins stay warm in the cold water.

 Deep at the bottom of the ocean, the **floor** is very dark. Not much sunlight reaches it. It's not easy to live here, either.

People can travel deep underwater in special vehicles called submersibles.

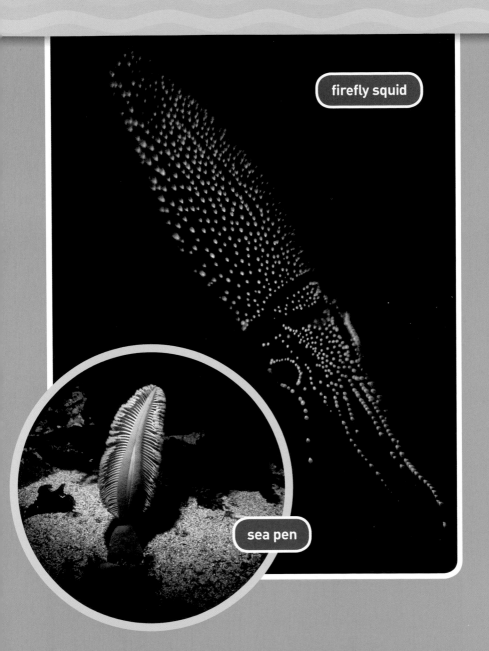

firefly squid

sea pen

Many critters live by the deep ocean **floor**. It is dark and cold, but it is still home.

YOUR TURN!

Match the animal to where it lives.

A

B

C

ANSWERS:
A-2
B-3
C-1

CHAPTER 3

Animals in the Ocean

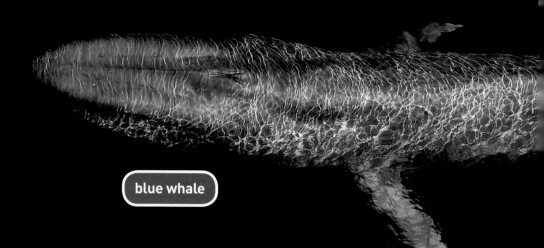

blue whale

There are many kinds of ocean animals: big and small, fast and slow! The blue whale is the biggest animal on Earth. It doesn't hunt big fish, though. Instead, it scoops up **tiny** animals called plankton.

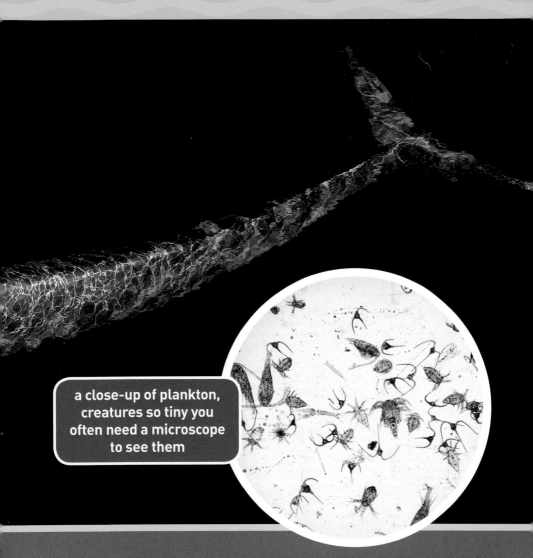

a close-up of plankton, creatures so tiny you often need a microscope to see them

There are lots of **tiny** animals in the ocean! Some are so small you can't see them with just your eyes.

YOU READ Some animals can live **deep** in the ocean. Yeti crabs and tube worms live near underwater volcanoes. Anglerfish hunt for food near the ocean floor.

anglerfish

 Other animals can't swim very **deep**. Seahorses stay in shallow water.

YOU READ

Manatees drift slowly under the water. They don't have to be **fast**. They have plenty of food to eat, and no animals hunt them.

Other animals are **fast** swimmers. This fish is one of the fastest animals in the ocean.

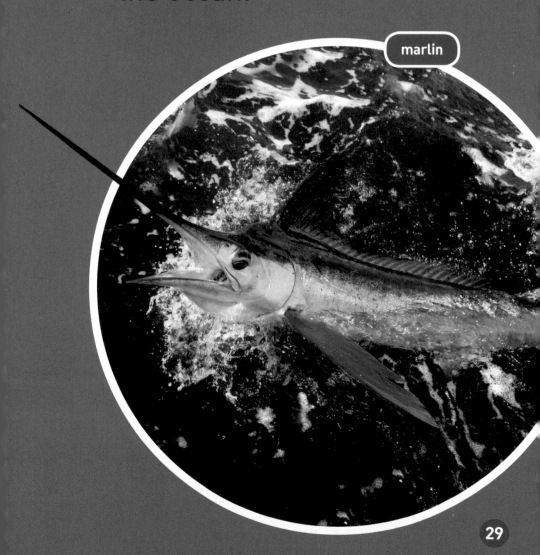

marlin

YOU READ Jellyfish have **soft** bodies. Some types of jellyfish protect themselves with their tentacles. If an animal gets too close, the tentacles will sting it!

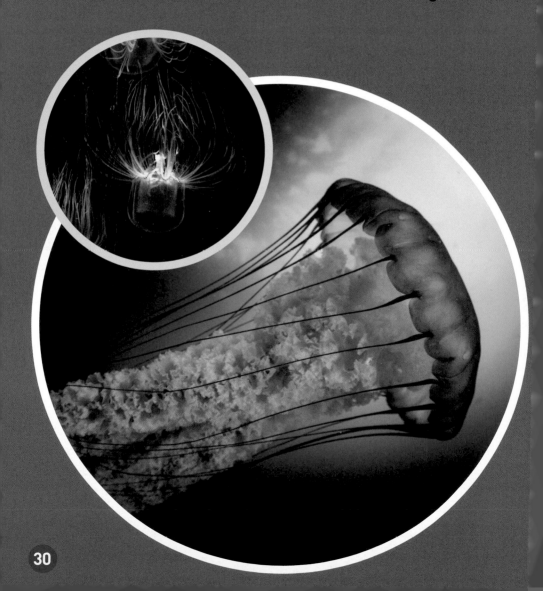

 This turtle has a hard shell. It keeps the turtle's **soft** body safe.

YOU READ

This slug has a **colorful** body. Its bright colors are a warning for other animals. They mean that this slug is poisonous. If an animal eats the slug, it could get sick.

This fish is hard to see! It is not **colorful**. Its color helps it hide in the sand.

flounder

YOUR TURN!

Draw an animal you might see in the ocean. Tell about the animal you drew.

Is it big or small?

Hard or soft?

Colorful or not colorful?

CHAPTER 4

People and the Ocean

 YOU READ

People all over the world use the ocean for work and for play. Boats like this one **carry** people out on the ocean to catch fish.

 Big ships **carry** cargo. This ship will travel to another part of the world.

YOU READ

Many people **enjoy** relaxing on the beach. Others glide over the waves on surfboards.

I READ People swim in the ocean, too. They **enjoy** seeing the animals that live there.

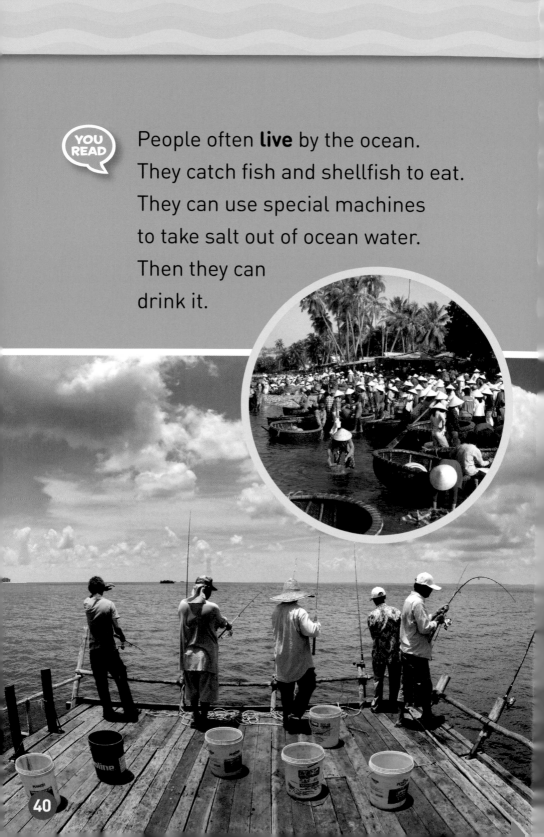

People often **live** by the ocean.
They catch fish and shellfish to eat.
They can use special machines
to take salt out of ocean water.
Then they can
drink it.

 Some people **live** in tall houses on stilts. The stilts keep water from getting inside.

 YOU READ

Most of Earth's water is in the ocean. Many animals and plants live there. Many people live near it, too. That's why it's important to **protect** the ocean.

 You can **protect** the ocean by keeping it clean.

When people litter, the trash they drop on the ground can end up in the ocean. Trash in the ocean can make people and animals sick. You can **help** by picking up trash on the beach.

You can also **help** by learning as much as you can. Share what you know! Then other people can help the ocean, too.

YOUR TURN!

Pretend you are by the ocean. Tell a story about what you are doing.

For my parents. —J.S.

Designed by YAY! Design

The author and publisher gratefully acknowledge the expert content review of this book by Dr. Danielle Dixson, University of Delaware, School of Marine Science and Policy, and the literacy review by Kimberly Gillow, principal, Milan Area Schools, Michigan.

Paperback ISBN: 978-1-4263-3235-7
Reinforced library binding ISBN: 978-1-4263-3236-4

Illustration Credits

Cover, Jeff Hunter/Getty Images; 1, Willyam Bradberry/Shutterstock; 3, Darlyne A. Murawski/National Geographic Creative; 4-5, Arrangements-Photography/Getty Images; 5, leonello/Getty Images; 6, Mykolastock/Shutterstock; 7, Lilly Trott/Shutterstock; 8-9, Kirill Umrikhin/Shutterstock; 9, Elenathewise/Getty Images; 10 (LE), Inti St Clair/Getty Images; 10 (RT), jhorrocks/Getty Images; 11 (UP), FatCamera/Getty Images; 11 (LO LE), antikainen/Getty Images; 11 (LO RT), People-Images/Getty Images; 12, Christophe Courteau/Nature Picture Library; 13, James Caldwell/Alamy Stock Photo; 14, Michael Zeigler/Getty Images; 15 (UP), Brian J. Skerry/National Geographic Creative; 15 (LO), jeanro/Getty Images; 16-17, johnandersonphoto/Getty Images; 17, BrianLasenby/Getty Images; 18, Paul Nicklen/National Geographic Creative; 19, Paul Nicklen/National Geographic Creative; 20, Brian J. Skerry/National Geographic Creative; 21 (LE), Jeff Rotman/Nature Picture Library; 21 (RT), David Liittschwager/National Geographic Creative; 22 (UP), Rich Carey/Shutterstock; 22 (LO LE), Neil Aronson/Shutterstock; 22 (LO RT), StevenRussellSmithPhotos/Shutterstock; 23 (UP), Bryan Toro/Shutterstock; 23 (CTR), Vlad61/Shutterstock; 23 (LO), lovleah/Getty Images; 24-25, Chase Dekker/Shutterstock; 25, blickwinkel/Alamy Stock Photo; 26, David Shale/Nature Picture Library; 27, Alex Mustard/Nature Picture Library; 28, Carol Grant/Getty Images; 29, Tono Balaguer/Shutterstock; 30 (UP), Gino Santa Maria/Shutterstock; 30 (LO), Velvetfish/Getty Images; 31, Andrey Armyagov/Shutterstock; 32, DaveBluck/Getty Images; 33, subaquapix/Getty Images; 34-35 (artwork), Austin Tramel; 34-35 (crayons), Charles Brutlag/Dreamstime; 36, eurotravel/Getty Images; 37, zhudifeng/Getty Images; 38 (UP), Hero Images/Getty Images; 38 (LO), Epic-StockMedia/Shutterstock; 39, strmko/Getty Images; 40 (UP), Gavin Hellier/robertharding/Getty Images; 40 (LO), toonman/Getty Images; 41, imageBROKER/REX/Shutterstock; 42-43, Stocktrek Images/National Geographic Creative; 44, Rich Carey/Shutterstock; 44-45, AE Pictures Inc./Getty Images; 46-47, idream-photo/Shutterstock; header throughout, art-sonik/Shutterstock

National Geographic supports K–12 educators with ELA Common Core Resources.
Visit natgeoed.org/commoncore for more information.

Printed in the United States of America
18/WOR/1